Strengthen Your Brothers

50th Jubilee of Intercession for Priests

Fr. Jack Finnegan SDB DD & Fr. Kevin Scallon CM

Intercession for Priests

Copyright © [2025] by Intercession for Priests

All rights reserved.

No portion of this book may be reproduced in any form without written permission from the publisher or author, except as permitted by U.S. copyright law.

Contents

1. Kevin Scallon: A Kind of Spiritual Memoir   1
   By Fr. Jack Finnegan SDB DD
2. Intercession for Priest: From 16 July to 15 August 1976   31
   A Report by Fr. Kevin Scallon CM
3. Vessels of Clay   39
   Some Thoughts On The Priesthood by Fr. Kevin Scallon CM
4. Intercession for Priests: A Final Reflection   43
   By Fr. Kevin Scallon CM
5. 50 Years of Intercession for Priests   45
   A Visual Celebration

Chapter 1

Kevin Scallon: A Kind of Spiritual Memoir

By Fr. Jack Finnegan SDB DD

I first met Kevin Scallon personally in 1976 at the first gathering of the Intercession for Priests, which Kevin had founded, with the support of his brother Vincentian Fr Myles Rearden. I remember the occasion well. I joined the group in the afternoon of the first day following a phone call from a fellow student in Rome, Fr Trevor Trotter, an Australian Columban on holiday in Ireland. I still remember Trevor's message, how succinct and to the point it was: *Get down here quick. There is something important happening, something prophetic*! Trevor, who has spent much of his own life working with priests, teaching scripture, and in leadership with the Columbans, never spoke a truer word and was present at the Intercession for several years while he was this side of the world.

That first meeting is sharply etched in my memory: a small group of priests praying together and sharing their spiritual desires and experiences, most of them involved with the Charismatic Renewal at the time. The atmosphere was electric. The sense of the Spirit's radiant presence was palpable, and Kevin sat there smiling, a seeming island of peace, wisdom and tranquility in our midst. I learnt afterwards that he was in fact quite anxious that day, concerned for the success of a venture that he was convinced was born of God. Several years later it was common for us to have more than a hundred priests concelebrating Mass together during the Intercession.

The message I have held onto since that first day has been central to my own ministry ever since and allows the charism of the Intercession to shine through. Our call as priests is to share the story of God's awesome love with the whole world. We are to be love bearers, life bearers, peace bearers to all in need. Jesus is with us always, inspiring and opening ever-new ways to the healing and transformation of lives. As Kevin frequently reminded us, we are Jesus Christ in the power of the Spirit. The challenge is to live what is a unitive life in a gently loving, coherent manner, proclaiming that Jesus is risen, that Jesus lives: in a word, ordinary mystics in everyday life.

In effect, the priest is called to be a transcendent point of reference in an increasingly secular, disbelieving and materialistic world. That is why the Intercession for Priests has become a necessity in a Church in dire crisis born of the vile behaviour of various priests and bishops. For Kevin, a renewal of the priesthood was –and is – imperative today and a clear vision of a path of spiritual and pastoral renewal forms the charismatic heart of the Intercession as Kevin understood it, something grounded in a constantly renewed commitment to a transformative rhythm of prayer, reflection, service, and engaged contemplation. Kevin knew that a spirituality that is not practised is not real.

What Kevin had at the back of his mind is easily summarised. First, priesthood is a way of holiness. It bespeaks a unitive experience of the living Christ, the graced capacity to step beyond the polarised, conflicted and dualistic universe in which we tend to live. Who is mystically present when we say, *This is my body, my blood given for you*? What are the transformative and self-transcending implications of engaging in such ritual and sacramental actions? After all, as St Paul reminds us, Christ is not divided (1 Corinthians 1:13). Second, when speaking of priests, Kevin was fond of quoting two well-known phrases in Latin from the spiritual tradition, *alter Christus* and *in persona Christi* that make the same point. He saw the priesthood from a position of a lifelong commitment to oneness with Christ.

Kevin was convinced that moral relativism has no part to play in the life of the priest. I came across a pertinent quote in Bishop Robert Barron's recent *Letter to a Suffering Church* (Park Ridge, IL: Word on Fire, 2019). I recommend this little book to all who are concerned about the state of the Church not just in the USA, but in the West. Bishop Barron writes: A priest whose central preoccupation is money or pleasure or power or career advancement or fame will, sooner or later, fall apart and wreak havoc around him. Those of us who have been involved with the Intercession over the years have no difficulty acknowledging the truth of the Bishop's observation. A soul search on St. Peter's stance will make the point: *You are living stones that God is building into his spiritual temple. What's more, you are his holy priests. Through the mediation of Jesus Christ you offer spiritual sacrifices that please God* (1 Peter 2:5).

Two stories about Kevin come to mind. The first dates back to Kevin's time as a missionary in Nigeria during the Biafran war. The story unfolds on an unexpectedly quiet Sunday morning when Kevin returned to his mission for breakfast after several Masses at out-stations. On his way into the house he was met by a frail young woman who had lost her husband and her three young children to the diseases and hunger rampant at the time. Feeling a little tired and put out, Kevin did what he could, asking his catechist to put some things together for her. When she received what the catechist brought, she placed them on the ground and began to sing and dance around them. "What is she singing about?" Kevin asked. "She is thanking God for you" the catechist replied. Kevin then had a chat with the young woman about God and faith. What she said remained with him for the rest of his life: *For me, today, you are Jesus Christ.*

The second story is set on a hot and humid summer's day in Washington, DC. Kevin had gone to the cleaners to pick up his things, dressed for the weather in T-shirt, shorts and sandals. As the shop assistant, a Caribbean woman, was handing him his change she asked, "Are you a priest?" When he asked her how she knew, she answered, *You have the mark of Jesus Christ on you.* Kevin's point is easily made. Encounters like these are moments of grace opening doors to change and transformation.

The more the priest encounters Christ, the more he prays and meditates, the more he will come to unity in Christ. The more he grows into union with Christ, the more he will experience the disintegration of his selfish ego and put on the compassionate gentleness and understanding humility of Jesus. Such is the transformative power of the Spirit. Such is the vastness of grace. Such is the power of the resurrection at work in a cosmos flowing towards its ultimate destiny in Christ. Such is the path of the everyday mystic. We need to be converted again and again to our priesthood.

Two stories will help to make the point. I remember on one occasion during the Intercession when Kevin invited Seamus Mulvaney, Diarmuid O'Riain, Pat Dwyer, Bonaventure Leahy and myself to go aside to pray and discern with him in preparation for a talk he was scheduled to give that evening. We gathered around Kevin and had just begun to pray when we were disturbed by two other priests who came into the room where we were. We did not recognise either of them. Anyway, they joined us, but the mood had changed and at a signal from Kevin we began to pray for the two strangers. In true charismatic style, the two of them slumped gracefully to the floor, allowing us to finish praying with Kevin. We then ministered to the two and discovered that both were priests in the grip of powerful addictions, one to alcohol and the other to prescription drugs. Both were healed and one of them went on to play a role in the Intercession in England.

The other story involves two Irish priests who booked into the Intercession but with the intention of going to the races at Leopardstown near Dublin. They were simply looking for somewhere to stay. However, they never got to the races, joining with their brother priests in prayer. They had what St John Paul II called a personal encounter with the risen Christ and attended the Intercession for more than a few years. Life truly begins for the priest when he personally meets God.

Kevin had been readied for his work with priests through his earlier ministry as a missionary in Nigeria, as a retreat leader, and as a spiritual director in seminaries in Ireland and abroad. The Intercession did not come out of the blue! It evolved as Kevin grew not only in his understanding of priesthood but also in his awareness of its existential and spiritual needs. As an experienced spiritual director, he was, for example, a founder member of AISGA, the national association of spiritual directors in Ireland.

The three scripture texts Kevin eventually chose to ground the Intercession are interesting. Sit with them. Use them for *lectio divina*. See where they take you.

- *Simon, behold Satan desired to have you that he might sift you like wheat, but I have prayed for you that your faith may not fail; and when you have turned again, strengthen your brethren* (Luke 22:31-32).
- *In the days of his flesh...Jesus offered up prayers and supplications with loud cries and tears... and was heard...*(Heb. 5:7).
- *Because Jesus lives forever, he has a permanent priesthood. Therefore he is able to save completely those who come to God through him, because he always lives to intercede for them* (Heb. 7:24-25).

Intercession and Worship

What I have to say here about intercession and worship has been honed in many conversations with Kevin Scallon. Intercession is a form of prayer that has at its heart an intentional opening to God's loving and liberating presence in the world. At its best, intercessory prayer is worship-saturated. In fact, as our three texts make clear, Christ's primary role as high priest is to make continual intercession for the people. A wonderful picture of worship-saturated intercession is painted in Revelations 5:8-10: *When he had taken the scroll, the four living creatures and the twenty-four elders fell before the Lamb, each holding a harp and golden bowls full of incense, which are the prayers of the saints.* Harp and bowl in hand, worship magnifies God by challenging and changing our perception of God. It is not difficult to see the link to priestly prayer and spirituality.

Worship demands a big heart and a big mind fit for the vastness of God. The intercessor's view of God is big! It is Christ-like, full of the

Spirit, focused unashamedly on the limitless power of God's love to change lives. It knows the Father as the Merciful, the Compassionate. It knows Christ as the Beloved Saving One, the Teacher, the Healer. It knows the Spirit as the Wind, the Breath, the Light, the Fire. The truth is that intercession opens up our vision of God and expands it. Try it and find out! Discover what Jesus said in Luke 6:38: *The measure with which you measure will be measured out to you.* Worshipful intercession is prayer full of awareness of human neediness and fragility and God's vast compassion. It is prayer seeking to make a difference.

How big, how abundantly lavish is God in my personal experience and understanding? How open is my mind, my heart? How judgmental, or rigid, or restricted, or spiritually stingy? Can I sing with the psalmist (Psalm 34:3): *Oh, magnify the Lord with me, and let us exalt His name together*! Can I sing the same words with Mary as she visits Elizabeth? Both psalmist and Mary knew that they could not make God big, but they could let their own vision grow and expand and develop. They understood God's lavish love poured out, full measure, pressed down, shaken together, and running over (Luke 6:38). They discovered how to see God big, lavish, abundant, beyond measure (see 1 John 3:1). Do I? Or is the smallness of my vision one of the reasons why my worship – and my leadership of worship – is so often so flat?

Just as holiness expands us, intercession challenges us to go beyond our limited and limiting ego-centred visions, the self-made dream-worlds we confuse with reality. Holiness enlarges our image of God. It widens our perception. It gives us insight into the heart of Christ. It allows us to glimpse the creative fire of Spirit flowing through the universe. Holiness means that we have been touched by the fires of saving grace. That is how intercession enables us to be part of something more than any ego can imagine. It liberates us from our reactive, self-centred dreams. It frees us from our defensive illusions.

No wonder that at the Intercession for Priests we begin each morning by welcoming those who have arrived and praying with them for the three gifts of the Intercession: a listening heart, the gift of intercession itself, and a great love for the priesthood.

Intercession is a profoundly biblical form of prayer for others. It involves standing in the broken places of people's lives and bringing their needs to God. The focus shifts intentionally from self to pray in favour of someone else. We stand in God's presence intervening in favour of our brothers and sisters. A great example of the intercessor is found in the story of Job who intercedes for his family and for his three friends (Job 1:5; 42:7-10). If you sit for a moment with the story in chapter 42 you will see how Job's intercession becomes a turning point of change. Consider Abraham as an intercessor (Genesis 17:18; 18:23-32). We see it in the life and ministry of Moses (see for example Exodus 17), and it is there at the beginning of the Church when the faith community in Jerusalem prayed for Peter's release from prison (Acts 12:1-18).

At the Intercession for Priests we have witnessed such turning points, such pivotal moments in many lives over many years. There is something mystical about intercession, something of the mystery of grace, something deeply experiential and transformative. And that transformation does not stop with the individual priest. When the pastor's faith and spirituality start to blossom so does the local faith community. In our experience intercession for priests and pastors moves the quality of ministry onto a higher plane.

This should come as no surprise since intercession always assumes a loving encounter with the living God. And for Kevin, worship-saturated intercession lay at the heart of priestly life and prayer, at the very heart of Word and Eucharist. He knew that intercession is a fundamental expression of both true worship and true devotion. After all, he had woven intercession into the very warp and woof of his own spirituality and ministry for many years. In fact, intercession informed his ecclesiology.

These are just some of the ideas about the interweaving of holiness and intercession and worship Kevin and I explored down the years in our conversations at night, often over a glass of wine, during the Intercession in All Hallows. Remembering those conversations brings to mind a question from one of Rumi's poems:

And you?
When will you begin that long journey into yourself?

It also brings to mind the pathos of God's complaint about priests and prophets in Ezekiel 22:23-30, *And I sought for anyone among them who would repair the wall and stand in the gap before me on behalf of the land, so that I would not destroy it; but I found no one*. If the priest is not spiritually alive, if the priest is not ready to stand in the gap, is it any wonder if the faith community suffers? When we pray for priests and bishops we are praying for the faith community itself. The point is made abundantly clear in the story of another great Old Testament intercessor, Esther, who stood in the gap for a whole people. Priests need to be converted afresh to priesthood and the needs of the faith community.

The Way of Conversion

Kevin often spoke about conversion. But his vision was much more broadly spiritual than might be expected: a change of mind is much broader than a change of sin. And that change of mind towards God was his goal. As a son of St Vincent he spoke caringly and often about his founder's own layered conversion, to the poor, to the priesthood, to the holy, a form of what in spirituality is termed the second or adult conversion, or in Pentecostal language, the baptism in the Spirit, a profound renewal of faith and love that takes us far beyond self-image and survival needs: a need felt even by great saints. It is a conversion to all that is, an openness to everything and nothing, to the very paradox of reality as we encounter it. In fact, Kevin saw a form of St Vincent's conversion to the poor in what today we would describe as conversion to a world and a planet in distress.

These are radical existential and experiential changes that Kevin confronted in himself before he ever confronted others with their reality. Conversion at this level is about radical change, change at the deepest levels of human and Christian identity. What is more fundamental for a priest than conversion to the infinite, to the vast variety of reality as it presents itself to us in ever new and unexpected ways? At such moments we discover that love is all. How easy it is for us to forget that our homeland is always becoming, always ending, always starting anew. Conversion to the priesthood inevitably involves conversion to change.

These were conversions Kevin himself experienced. He was converted to the poor in Biafra, an essential moment in his Vincentian journey. He was converted to the priesthood in a variety of encounters with people, an essential moment in what was to become the Intercession for Priests and his wider ministry. He lived himself what he helped so many other priests to experience. We all need such a conversion and Kevin was a living example of what that looks like. Kevin knew that genuine spirituality is self-implicating of its very nature. It is lived gospel. So is priesthood. My spirituality is the spiritual story I tell; and it makes no sense if it is largely theoretical, an unlived fiction or a defensive illusion. What could be more important than singing our story with the Spirit? What could be more important than listening to God?

Kevin listened to God in all kinds of ways, in scripture, in nature, in other people's stories, in theatres, in palaces, in hovels, in out of the way places, and in times of silence and prayer. He heard it in voices of need and in voices of critique, and in the listening his own story changed and emerged and his sense of humour flourished. Kevin knew that God sings his sacred tale through many different stories – some funny, some sad– weaving tapestries of wonder and surprise. God is all in all (Ephesians 4:6), a tree with the trees, a flower with the flowers, a raindrop with raindrops, a friend with a friend in ways many of us never grasp. That is why I am not surprised that Kevin's friends included comedians and bishops, singers and cardinals, presidents and kings. But that's another tale for another day!

I remember a story Kevin told a few of us one afternoon that makes the point. It seems he was somewhere in England leading a silent retreat on prayer in a centre which had the local parish-priest for lunch each day. So Kevin was invited to share lunch in the parlour with the parish-priest. In the course of conversation the priest asked Kevin about the theme of the retreat and Kevin told him. It turned out that the priest was very interested in the theme of prayer and had many books on the subject! Those who new Kevin's wry humour can guess what happened next. Like a good spiritual director Kevin posed the key question: When are you going to begin? I wonder still how the poor man took Kevin's smiling query. But the point is well-made. Prayer and spirituality are only real if they are practised. They are about how and why we live as we do.

There is another conversion that Kevin lived profoundly: a kind of baptism or conversion to wonder. I suspect the root of this conversion was in his devotion to Mary, shaped by the music of the Rosary, honed in the Stations of the Cross, and grounded in her Magnificat. The lilting strains and themes of Mary's song of praise echo brightly in

Kevin's spirituality and ministry. *My soul magnifies the Lord and my spirit rejoices in God my Saviour* (Luke 1:46)! For Kevin there was a message here for every Christian, a message for every priest: a challenge and an invitation too, a rhythm for life and a song for the journey in good times and bad.

What is at work in Mary's Magnificat is a conversion to wonder, the wonder of life, the wonder of birth, the wonder of beginnings, of hill journeys and family greetings, of babies leaping in wombs. The spirituality of the Magnificat enshrines a call to be more than a disciple, the call to be an everyday mystic. Such a spirituality challenges us to be joyful witnesses to God's breath-taking wonders. It should come as no surprise, then, that Kevin served as international spiritual director of *Magnificat*, a ministry to Catholic women born of the Charismatic Renewal, from 2001 until his death in 2018. Nor should it come as a surprise that he worked with Sr. Briege McKenna for more than forty years. Together they modelled a distinctly practical Christology, a compassionate Trinitarian vision, a love for Eucharist, full of care, full of healing, full of an empowering word, a loving blessing and an encouraging smile.

I saw another conversion unfold in Kevin over the years I knew him, a conversion to stillness and deep contemplative silence, a place where Kevin learnt to listen with the ears of the heart. This is something else he shared with his founder, Vincent de Paul. Like Vincent, Kevin was a man of practical and concrete work: ministering, preaching, teaching, writing and travelling in service of the word of life, especially in priests and people in need. But it reverberated with distinct undertones of contemplative silence, a transformed empathy, a kind of unpretentious, kindly, considerate, gentle yet firm fidelity to the will of God. Kevin's way was experiential, always open to a living God: a mystic heart made visible in a smile.

The Way of Silence and Trinity

Kevin knew that silence is something alive. It is neither an absence nor a gap. It is a living presence. Silence is not something to study; it is something to enter. It gifts us with the ability to sit quietly with truth, with beauty and goodness. It opens windows onto the sacred and the divine. It beckons us to walk like John of the Cross in fields of silent music. Like contemplation, silence is a mode of being, a quality of intimacy, an experience rather than a concept. It pierces illusion and discovers reality. That is why he emphasised it.

Silence draws us to the Father. It unfolds in the presence of the Comforter. It walks dusty roads in interweaving rhythms of compassionate service after the manner of Jesus. It listens without judgment. In contemplative silence God is here and now: presence, presencing, present, alive; and the mystic soul is attuned to God's love alive in the reality of the moment. Being and doing walk together in this vision of stillness and service, of silence and care, in the liberty of the Spirit becoming one with Christ. And that brings us to Kevin's Trinitarian vision.

The presence of the Trinity shines through Kevin's own writing. This is very clear in the first chapter of his book, *I Will Come Myself*. Describing his own experience Kevin refers to moments of grace and goes on to say that *the importance of such moments is not in words; it is experienced in the soul, the dwelling place of the Holy Trinity*. Kevin does not develop a theology here. His concern is practical, to describe a Trinitarian way, a way of transformative presence alive in the depths of every person's life.

The Father, Jesus Christ, the Spirit are encountered as friends, companions on the journey, helpers in the vicissitudes of life as the stories in this little book make clear. Like the kingdom, the Trinity is at hand, near, within, carried on the winds of love. The Trinity is pivotal and transformative in Kevin's experience. In the light of the Trinity everything becomes sacred, everything comes alive in an overflow of communion and loving presence. The Trinity is about communion, about an abundance of life, an abundance of love flowing freely into the world. Trinity is about the full flowering of life, of being, the full flowering of communion, the full flowering of love, justice and peace.

Our call is to be channels of that loving flow, that cosmic intimacy flowering in the hidden depths of things. To do otherwise is to embrace a stunted, inhibiting vision, one in which language itself is often twisted and turned against itself. What is happening to us when the intentional destruction of rain forests driven by greed is called development? When moral relativism is called freedom? If we subvert the truth how can we be free? Hence, a liberating, healing Christ who says, *I will come myself*. This is the Christ Kevin knew.

We are implicated with Trinity and as a consequence what happens to the outer world happens to the inner. The result of the absence of Trinity is an increasingly shallow, superficial, even vicious life, a life moved by greed not love, by violence not integrity. We stand at a crossroads making choices that have real consequences for Christian spirituality. When the outer world is lessened in its rich diversity and beauty why be surprised if the language of spirit is diminished, if the rich imaginative, emotional, and spiritual wisdom of the human family is steadily quenched. Kevin saw the signs of these things in his travels, especially in the lives of the poor. He witnessed their impacts and grieved.

Too often the busy priest lets go of Trinity. Leave it to the theologians, he might say. But Trinity is foundational to any genuine understanding of priesthood. This is not the place to go into the issue in depth, but some hints drawn from memories of Kevin's conversations, talks and homilies may prove helpful and necessary. Sit with each and let them question your understanding of priesthood. Trinity is relational. Is my ministry relational? Trinity mirrors joyful intimacy. Is my ministry touched by the joy of the Spirit? Trinity evokes the language of surrender. Whose will truly moves my ministry?

Trinity bespeaks gracious self-knowledge and self-acceptance. How does my inner world, my wants and needs, my hurts and drives, my habitual reactions, impact my ministry? Trinity opens us to the reality of dynamic Indwelling Love. Is my ministry rooted and shaped in the creative dance of such unifying Love? Trinity is passionate mission. Is my soul on fire? Does my priesthood reflect Trinity? Do I understand that Trinity is the fundamental grammar of all priestly forms of spirituality? Do I intentionally allow Trinity to orient all my relationships with the faith community? Do I understand Trinity as a life orienting transforming gift? Do I seek to live in the *imago Trinitatis*?

For Trinity is the Living Spring from which all creative life and love ultimately flow. No wonder that Gregory of Nyssa saw Trinity as a beautiful image cluster: the Anointer, the Anointed One and the Anointing. Or consider Julian of Norwich's image clusters: Might, Wisdom, Love; Joy, Bliss, Delight; Maker, Keeper, Lover; Fatherhood, Motherhood, Lord. Gerald O'Collins draws attention to another set of image clusters: Lover, Beloved, Equal Friend; Eternal Lover, Divine Beloved, Empowering Friend.

Trinity challenges the priest to go deep into the implications of and live an image of the Divine that confronts all Christians with the dynamism of loving availability, the mutuality of reciprocal love, and compassionate self-giving. Freedom grows as intimacy with God grows, as Trinitarian Love touches the very basis of our being. Trinity challenges all of us to hold the paradox of equality and difference, of origin and destiny, close to our hearts. It challenges us to be creative, healing, and empowering in all our dealings with people.

There is no room in trinitarian spirituality for power plays or games of rank and status, much less for the games of manipulation and collusive domination that have plagued the Church in recent decades. Trinity confronts us with a different way forward for the human spirit, a way of love, of respect, of integrity and truth. In a spirituality where the self is understood relationally rather than in isolation change happens. It is all too easy to forget that grace is the life of the Trinity touching the world, drawing it to a beautiful and lavishly generous future.

Like all Christian spirituality, priestly spirituality is dared to dance in terrains of depth and mystery, of generosity and beauty, to the music of Trinitarian Love. This is a love that seeks the good of all people and of all creation. It is such graced seeking that makes us God's special treasure (Deuteronomy 7:6) and fills us with a yearning to glimpse the glorious light of the Trinity in the loving face of Christ (2 Corinthians 4:6). A trinitarian spirituality also teaches us that love must blossom as service in the world or lose its essential Christian imprint.

It is the loving presence of Trinity that makes Christian – and priestly – spirituality an ongoing, ever deepening, ever descending and ascending, ever graceful, ever renewing, ever healing and creative process. The result is that genuine priestly ministry unfolds in a communion of friendship and compassion big enough for a cosmos. When the priest seeks to be spiritually awake and aware, he begins to sense the Trinitarian dance constantly making and remaking the world. He witnesses the Trinity making and remaking lives. He hears God calling priests and prophets to walk through the land. He understands St Paul's promise, *I will dwell in them and walk among them; and I will be their God, and they shall be My people* (2 Corinthians 6:16). He becomes alert to the ways Trinity seeks to make a loving home in us as Jesus promised (John 14:23). And Kevin Scallon spoke with love of all these things.

The Everyday Mystic

The question I encountered most frequently when I talked to others who knew Kevin and his spiritual vision was this: was Kevin Scallon a mystic? The answer to that question depends on how the mystical is described. The problem is that the word means so many different things to so many different people. *Mystic* is an elusive catch-all word if ever there was one, and it easily eludes precise definition. It can refer to someone who is crazy just as easily as to someone who is profoundly spiritual. And I have even seen ads for a mystic cat shop! And we have all seen references to mystic beauty.

When Karl Rahner wrote that the Christian of the twenty-first century would be a mystic or nothing, he was not talking about enclosed monastics. Rahner was thinking of ordinary people with jobs and families, of apostolic religious men and women, and priests trying to serve their faith communities in difficult times. As a good Ignatian he was thinking of people who were and are seeking to be engaged contemplatives in the world. Our concern here, then, is with engaged mysticism, the kind that moves you to go out and do your level best for the people of God, that motivates you to be the best kind of Christian lay person, religious, or priest you can be.

Anyone who knows the life of St Vincent de Paul will know that he was not a fan of extraordinary mystical phenomena. Yet he was a mystic. And if we are to describe Kevin as a mystic it will be in the same manner that his founder was a mystic: a mysticism that draws us out onto the street with the poor and needy, a mysticism with the smell of the sheep about it. What does everyday mysticism look like? It looks like Kevin Scallon, it looks like all of those who are trying to be faithful to the living God and the people we are sent to serve.

If we take Francis de Sales' ecstasy of action, his ecstasy of life, seriously we will see that the fruit of mystical experience is always made visible in real lives. It always has a harvest (Matthew 7:16). In other words, the mystical experience, if it is real and coherent, is played out in ordinary life, the result of unifying love. The love of God becomes visible in the way the mystic lives, in the way the priest ministers or the teacher teaches. In the wisdom of unifying love we overcome the apparent opposition between contemplation and action. The task of the Intercession for Priests is to support and encourage this movement.

Our concern is with a life of lived Presence. An integral life. A life of unifying love made flesh in the world. Our concern is with experiences that lift busy Christians into a place of oneness, into transforming personal encounters with the living God sending them out to serve. We live and move and have our being in the grace of unity (see Acts 17:28). More to the point, contemplate the experience of sharing fully in the paradoxically generative and kenotic energy of the Trinity as it gives itself away in love. This is the way of the everyday mystic.

Clues to the depth of such experiences are found not only in a priest's writing and homilies but more especially in their daily life and engagements, in their manner, their wisdom, their gentleness and consideration of others. And such experiences are commonly linked to a life of prayer, to meditation, spiritual reading, sharing God's word, and a range of spiritual actions and exercises moved by love and centred on God: bright flowers in a dappled garden of rich spiritual practices.

Everyday mysticism is best described as a synthesis of many ways. First of all, let us describe it as a way of paradox. Anyone who takes Jesus at his word and seeks to go beyond the bare minimum inevitably encounters the paradox of life in an ever-changing world. Consider how faith speaks of a Presence felt yet still to come. There is a self to be renounced and transcended. More, in the gospels Jesus is a Master of paradox, and the Christian mystic is one who seeks to live the Christian paradox according to the mind of Christ. If you would be first be last. If you would save your life you must lose it. The alpha is the omega. The God who is present is the God who is absent. Paradox is there in our key doctrines: in the Trinity, in the incarnation, in grace. And then there is the dance of order and chaos in the cosmos of which we are a part.

The purpose of paradox in spirituality has little or nothing to do with logic or problem solving. It has everything to do with liberating us from the limits of the rational mind. The rational mind believes it is able to solve all problems. It does not recognise that it is a prisoner of language and its oppositional thinking, the kind of stubborn or self-righteous thinking that so often leads to conflicts and wars. Every quarrel, every conflict, every war multiplies in a nasty nest of power-driven oppositional thinking.

Mystics on the way of paradox intuit this and seek a different way, the way of unifying love. They seek to recognise and move through oppositional thinking and beyond it, a difficult task at the best of times. Can you recognise the powerful impact of socio-religious and socio-political conditioning in your own stances and behaviours? The everyday mystic seeks a place of union in Christ. He or she tries to see from a position of oneness, from a place that lets go of judgmental and condemnatory attitudes. And I am suggesting that Kevin was doing his best to struggle with such paradox, to let it bring him into a place of greater freedom. I know this from conversations with him. Living with paradox is not easy. Freedom from oppositional thinking and habitual reactions is not easy.

What is easy is to drop out of oneness, out of the grace of unity in Christ, and return to the oppositional thinking we learnt before we ever learnt sense. Oppositional thinking, saying no, disagreeing, is inbred in our defensive identities. Paradoxically, our spirituality wants us to say yes. There is a struggle here but there is also grace. Who completes this journey before they die? As St Therese of Lisieux wrote in her autobiography, *the storm thunders at my heart; I find it difficult to believe in the existence of anything except the clouds which limit my horizon*. But then we discover the possibilities of our weakness. Or as St Paul's paradox puts it, *When I am weak then I am strong* (2 Corinthians 12:10). Would you see Kevin Scallon there?

Part of the way of paradox is dealing with our own incompletion, our weakness, the fact that we are not finished even as we seek to embrace our ultimate destiny. Accepting everything, resisting nothing, led by the Spirit! There is a lot of dying to do before we die, a lot of wrestling with paradox before we come to the glory of oneness in Christ the Master of Paradox. He holds out to us an image of loving unity, an image of oneness that cuts through all the illusions of reality in which we tend to live, those dream-realities that have no real existence outside our own heads. In the paradox of Jesus we encounter the is-ness of all in a life lived on the edge. And this brings us to a second path: our commitment to awareness.

Ordinary mysticism is a way of awakening to something – someone – already there. What we awaken to is a presence and a journey, in biblical terms, the journey to Jerusalem, or climbing the holy mountain, or looking for Jacob's ladder, that ancient symbol of the journey between earth and heaven. Those of us who are not alert, who are not committed to awareness, all too easily fall into the ways of masculine thinking. We want to arrive. We want to get the job done. We want to be successful. The ordinary mystic recognises the traps hidden in these signals and cultivates patient awareness. What is important is to be on the way, to be faithful. Loving fidelity in the moment is the key. The everyday mystic is someone like Bartimaeus sitting going nowhere outside Jericho who, recognising Jesus passing by, jumps up, throws off the authority of his past, and follows Jesus (Mark 10:46-52).

There are echoes in this story of feminine spiritual symbolism. It is there in the embodied nature of the encounter. It is there in the existential reality of the moment and the concrete nature of the change that takes place. It is visible in the softening of stances and the change from rebuking to encouraging and nurturing. It is especially present in the receptive nature of the meeting and the new life that flows from it. Mind and heart are set on Christ. Other key qualities such as creative presence, being in relationship, process, intimacy and healing are also present. So is the capacity to see through the oppositional nature of language, its capacity to hide what I do not want to see or reveal. And so is the expansive and spacious presence of holiness.

Holiness is a work of God, a work of the Spirit building on nature, making us more than we are, gifting us for service. These are all qualities of the ordinary, everyday mystic, somebody who is open to being made more in a whole variety of ways, heart made bigger, more open, more receptive, more coherent, not to mention their discovery and revitalisation of soul and spirit. The human spirit is empowered to be more creative. The soul opens to new and deeper levels of wisdom.

Self-control grows and the fruit of the Spirit blossoms. Holiness makes us real as followers of Christ. We become mirrors of the One we serve, less limited and less limiting. We empower those we serve. We do not hinder or limit them to suit our own – often unrecognised, often subtle – ego-centric power needs. The everyday mystic wrestles with such forces, works through them and seeks to offer a more loving, more considerate response. Take the story of Moses. He was called to live a life of responsibility to God. But he was also called to live all of this in his own particularity. He was called to stand in the centre of his own story. I have seen a similar process at work in Kevin Scallon.

Another way of talking about the way of awakening is to understand it as a way of conversion, the way of a repentant heart, the touch of metanoia. It is the way of Third Isaiah: *But this is the one to whom I will look, to the humble and contrite in spirit, who trembles at my word* (Isaiah 66:2).This is David's way, the way of a humbled, contrite heart (Psalm 51:17). It is also the way of Jesus: Take my yoke upon you, and learn from me; for I am gentle and humble in heart, and you will find rest for your souls (Matthew 11:29). It is a way that embraces the paradox of change and transformation with humility and a contrite heart.

The nature of genuine awakening is clear in the story of Bartimaeus. It is the story of a blindman going nowhere who is overtaken by a seemingly chance divine encounter. The everyday mystic is someone like Bartimaeus who wakes up and embraces the way to Jerusalem, the way through the Cross to change and transformation. Who desires metanoia? He or she who is not yet finished but is on the way with Jesus. Like Bartimaeus they are awakening to something, to Someone. They wake up, they meet the living Christ and are liberated from all that went before. Something new comes to birth in them. They find something fresh in the present that sets them moving, and the Church moves with them. Paul calls it putting on the mind of Christ, a mind that is already there for us, a mind of openness and love, a mind that recognises failure and repents.

I think Kevin Scallon was a mystic in this sense. He was awake and he was on the way. He was receptive, doing what needed to be done, living his priesthood with a smile and a twinkle in his eye. He wrestled with paradox and accepted the challenge to be a better, freer, more open, more gentle, more kindly, more forgiving version of himself. He repented and forgave. He knew that without a commitment to humble awareness spirituality becomes detached from lived reality. In the awesome paradox of grace and freedom Kevin accepted Christ as his Teacher and Guide. And something new was brought to birth through his fidelity and service. In Mark's terms he was on the way with Jesus. In Luke's terms he took up his cross daily and sought to be faithful. He had a repentant spirit. If this isn't descriptive of the everyday mystic I don't know what is.

There are other ways of talking about everyday mysticism. It is a way of practice, a way that makes prayer and action and virtue real in the world. The mystic knows that prayer is not a concept. It is real only if we do it. The same is true of meditation. If we don't sit nothing much will happen. The same is true of service and action. They are all practices making fidelity and love real. You may have the deepest thoughts but without action they wither on the vine. They are seed on stony ground.

We know that Kevin was a man of prayer. We know he spoke knowingly and lovingly of it and wrote about it. We know that he wrote beautiful prayers. But what is most relevant is that he prayed. He prayed with the whole of his being. He journeyed into the depths of prayer: mind, heart, feelings, body and it shaped the whole of his life. Prayer is reality finding its way to God in us and through us, bringing us with it. Kevin knew that prayer grows out of our belief that God is Love. It reveals where we are in terms of our deepening faith, trust, entrustment and surrender to God. He knew that in prayer we stake everything on Jesus.

Much the same may be said about the way of service. Kevin didn't just write about service, he served, he was available, he accompanied and listened and prayed. Like the Good Samaritan he refused to pass on the other side. He was available. He empowered. He encouraged. He prayed for healing. He knew that gospel service unfolds right where you are at the moment. He remembered that spirituality is real only when it is lived and practiced. He put his contemplation into action and his prayer bore much fruit. Seen from this perspective I think it fair to say that Kevin Scallon was an everyday mystic.

We can also describe everyday mysticism as an emphasis on what is central and essential to the life of faith. And what is most essential is love. The everyday mystic is an active bearer of God's love in the world. What is love? Is it in the saying or doing? We see the mystic's love in the loving, in the doing, in the service, in the healing, empowerment and liberation its brings. Love is about being open, about being kind and gentle, about being generous and forgiving. If there isn't fire it isn't love, and to the mystic the fire says, Be strong! Live love!

Mystics are ready to go through the fire for those they serve. They understand that real love is ready to die for another. They know that love is the foundational, God-created energy in the cosmos. They know that love is greater than an ocean(Song of Songs 8:7). They know that love is a light in a darkened world and they bring that light with them wherever they go. Those who knew him felt this love in Kevin. More, they saw it in action and recognised Jesus at its bright core. This is not to say that Kevin was perfect. He was aware of his faults and repented them. He didn't like being criticised. He didn't like being told when things were not going well. Who does? But he listened because he sought completion in a loving Christ.

The everyday mystic doesn't like his or her own faults and failings. They recognise it, acknowledges it, work with it, and move ahead. They recognise, acknowledge, take responsibility for and let go of their habitual reactions. That is why the way of the everyday mystic is a way of continual conversion. Conversion is a change of mind, a change of heart, a change of behaviour that reveals the touch of holiness. Conversion considers more than how my sin works. It seeks to recognise and understand how my mind works – and how my unconscious mind works– because it is concerned in grace for the Spirit-sown seeds of holiness and wholeness.

I do not know what my unconscious mind is doing. But others do. They see it in my face. They hear it in the tone of my voice. They see it in my movements and gestures. If I am not open to criticism, to correction and challenge, how am I to truly know myself? If I do not listen to others how am I to know when I have become a prisoner of my own unconscious? How else may I come to know that I have been an all-unaware servant of my false self? What we do not know about ourselves controls us. The stuff I am hiding from God controls me.

That is why the everyday mystic seeks to understand the dance of awareness and unawareness. They seek out more awareness. They take responsibility. They listen to the whispers of Spirit. They understand that conversion allows barren places to become fruitful. It allows the seeds of holiness to be sown and watered in grace, and then find root and produce fruit at the proper time (Psalm 1:2-3).The everyday mystic takes care of these Spirit-sown seeds in themselves and others. They seek God's loving will. They remember what Paul wrote in Galatians 6:9, *Let us not become weary in doing good, for at the proper time we will reap a harvest if we do not give up*. Kevin did not give up. He helped so many to find their way back. He often spoke about these matters. I wonder what his harvest looks like.

There are still other ways in the everyday mystic's toolkit: the way of discipleship, the way of dealing with times that are changing for the worst. In fact, mysticism tends to flourish at times of change. Times of change and times of scandal also ground the way of radical prophecy, the way of disturbing the status quo, of stepping out of unquestioned or collusive mainstream thinking, of glib and intolerant political correctness and questionable ideology.

I hear echoes of Kevin in each of these. I hear him encouraging us to take a stance, to stand for something more significant, more honest, more bountiful. I hear him encouraging us to pray and meditate if only because prayer and meditation will confront us with what needs to change in ourselves and the Church. The everyday mystic is always ready to be disturbed by what needs to change in both the inner and the outer world.

Kevin also emphasised the way of the sacraments, especially the sacraments of initiation and the priesthood. He talked and wrote about them in ways that brought out their wholesomeness and beauty, the way they change lives. He also loved scripture as all mystics do. He was at home in the word of God. He could preach on the word of God at the drop of a hat! I know many priests were amazed at the depth of his insights. It was obvious that he spent quality time doing what today we call *lectio divina*.

And he had a habit of giving gifts of the Bible. I have no doubt that scripture took him to a place of deep contemplation and deep contemplation brought him to levels of insight that are unobtainable in any other way. No wonder he regularly invited scripture scholars like Francis Martin, may he rest in peace in God's glory, to come to the Intercession to break open the scriptures and let them come alive for those present.

Kevin loved good liturgy. He loved the beauty of it and the rhythms of it and invested time and money in providing for good music at the Intercession. Liturgy was the heart of his priesthood and the soul of his ministry. His mysticism was profoundly Eucharistic. He was a man of profound Eucharistic faith. Kevin believed that Eucharist is the nucleus of oneness with Christ and the Trinity. It is the door to unitive Love, the music of transformation. Kevin understood that the gift and challenge of union, of unitive Love, is there for every priest every time he celebrates Eucharist. The difficulty for many of us is that at the key moment of union, of consecration, we are distracted. The ego mind drifts off, but the mystic mind pulls us back. Which do we favour? Kevin loved bringing the Eucharist into people's lives. He favoured adoration. He favoured Eucharistic healing services, things any priest can do.

Kevin's mysticism was profoundly prayerful. He knew that prayer was a journey to the heart of God, a journey to the depths of stillness. Prayer starts with saying but ends up with being. This is the spiritual wonder of it, the beauty and the truth of it. He knew that the person sitting quietly and intentionally before God becomes a living prayer, every breath a song of praise, every glance full of gratitude. Prayer is openness to God. Prayer is receptivity to the Spirit come alive. Prayer is an encounter with truth and goodness drawn into the dance of Trinity, paradoxically open to presence and absence because the language that opposes one to the other is transcended in a profound quiet, an endless stillness. Sadly the human ego does not like such spaces and turns away. That is why the mystic learns to let ego and its wants go, not because the mystic is complete but because he or she hopes to be complete in Christ one day. It is a question of love cooperating with God.

The Christian mystic is a bearer of God's love to the world, a beacon of creative compassion amidst the chaos of the times. In effect, a mystic is in touch with reality, with her or his feet firmly on the ground. It should come as no surprise, then, that the approach favoured today, especially among active religious, is to understand the mystical in a broad, more inclusive sense, in a way that is descriptive of a life and commitment touched by and in touch with the sacred in every aspect of life and creation: recognising God in the world and bringing God to the world. It is an approach in which Julian of Norwich's famous dictum is easily remembered: *All shall be well, and all shall be well and all manner of things shall be well.*

In conversations with Kevin about the mystical, several aspects of the experience became clear. God is not passive in our experience. God, and the relationship with God is active, transformative, engaging. God is encountered as self-disclosing and self-identifying in ways that are awesome, direct and vivid, yet always challenging, always seeking to draw a life-giving yes from our instinctive no. From our perspective the encounter may be experienced as one-sided in the sense that it is unexpected, a surprise, an undeserved wonder, a vast gift, a marvel, a gentle touch of Spirit Breath. It makes us long for more.

The mystical is paradoxically complete and incomplete, in the sense that there is always more to come, to unfold, and to be encountered. There is room for growth. That is why the mystic today is an engaged mystic, a bright and active presence in the world's darkness, a peace-maker, a layer-on-of-hands, a speaker of healing words in spaces of conflict, the blessing of divine mercy among errant people, a builder of a better social-spiritual world touched by the living presence of God.

In the Irish tradition we always stand in a thin place, a *caol áit*, a place where the veil between us and the Holy becomes sheer and translucent: silence complete. We see it made plain in the story of Elijah running to save his life from Jezebel and encountering God at Horeb, the place where his calling turns (1 Kings 19:11-13). The story is worth repeating: *Now there was a great wind, so strong that it was splitting mountains and breaking rocks in pieces before the Lord, but the Lord was not in the wind; and after the wind an earthquake, but the Lord was not in the earthquake; and after the earthquake a fire, but the Lord was not in the fire; and after the fire a sound of sheer silence.*

When Elijah heard it, he wrapped his face in his mantle and went out and stood at the entrance of the cave. Then there came a voice to him that said, "What are you doing here, Elijah?"

And so we return to our opening question: was Kevin Scallon an engaged mystic? I think the answer is yes. The evidence is there for anyone who looks. In Kevin the Vincentian, what became evident is a deep interiority, a convinced faith-life that found both expression and nourishment in a life of committed and zealous action, qualities he shared with his founder, St Vincent de Paul. There is nothing abstract about Kevin's mysticism. Like Vincent's, Kevin's mysticism was essentially functional and practical, a mysticism of service and travel: he truly discovered the poor during the Biafran war. You can see the simplicity of it in his conversion to the poor and in his conversion to faith. It is clear in his conversion to the priesthood, of which the Intercession will hopefully be a lasting monument, and in his call to minister quietly to Christian leaders in Church and State around the world, as well as to Catholic royalty in Europe.

Kevin's life shows us a mystic with eyes open to see the needs of the world, heart and hands open to participation in all its anguish and tribulations. It is a way that walks in interweaving paths of prayer and service. It has clear social dimensions, something that is crystal clear in St Vincent's own mysticism of the poor and the oppressed. It is a way that is open to the Fatherhood of God, a blessing God lavish in holy surprises and gifts, opening doors and avenues we did not know were there. Kevin's is a way of active compassion, of radical belief in a God of mercy. It is a way that finds God in people and events as well as in quiet and the chapel. It is a way that knows how to listen and serve contemplatively. In fact, in my view Kevin's mystical experience was the true source of his action. As Francis de Sales once said, what we aim for is what we tend toward. And Love is always the key.

A Concluding Addendum

Why is a Salesian writing about a Vincentian? Let me conclude with two answers to this question. Kevin and I shared a co-accompanying relationship over more than forty years and so I think I can say that I know something of his spirituality and the ways he was moved by the Spirit. I could not have written what I have otherwise. But I had a second motive. St Vincent de Paul had a deep influence on the life of my own founder, Don Bosco. He caught the desire to work with poor and abandoned youth from Vincent. And Don Bosco worked with priests for many years. Few people today remember that Don Bosco also wrote and published a book of reflections on Vincent's spirituality with meditations for every day of a month; and he learnt from Vincent's engaged spirituality when he founded the Salesians. Don Bosco saw in Vincent the prototype of untiring charity and zeal. And something few Salesians know today. When the Salesian Rule was definitively published Don Bosco included in it a letter on community prayer written by Vincent on 15 January 1650 and there it stayed for more than seventy years. Both saints joined love as *affect* to love as *effect* and the world has reaped the benefits.

Chapter 2

Intercession for Priest: From 16 July to 15 August 1976

A Report by Fr. Kevin Scallon CM

In August, 1975 I visited the House of Prayer in Convent Station, New Jersey. It was an experience that, at the time, profoundly affected my life. At lunch on my first day there I sat beside a little Sister from somewhere in Latin America. She asked me if I had been to Bethany House. I had to tell her that I had not and, what was worse, that I had never heard of it. She enquired if I knew Fr. George Kosicki and I said yes, and that I had seen him at the Rome Conference and had bumped into him near the steps of the rostrum one day. We went on to talk about something else.

The same evening, I discovered in my room a copy of "Forty Day Intercession for Priests" by Frs. Gordon J. Judd, C.S.B. and George W. Kosicki, C.S.B. Inside were written the words "With Christ's love for you. Georgina." I have never seen or heard from Sr. Georgina since that day. So I read the booklet and thought it very interesting and was grateful that priests in America were receiving so much grace in that kind of way. I left the book down and never thought of it again until our Vincentian Provincial asked us to make suggestions about what new forms our annual retreats might take. It was during a conversation about this with my confrere and collaborator, Fr. Myles Rearden, that it came to us – why not a month of intercession for priests? I realise very clearly now that this idea had come not from ourselves but from the Spirit of the Lord. After that it was merely a question of seeking authorization where it was required and of asking for the approval of Dr. Ryan, the Archbishop of Dublin. From that time on I can say that the Lord gave me great assurance and peace that this would be His work and that He would see it completed. We drew up beautiful plans and themes for each week of the month and I am sure that the Lord must have smiled at us because when the time came His Holy Spirit dispensed with our plans and replaced them with more beautiful ones of His own. None of us objected.

And so on the 16th of July with a large empty house, an over-crowded schedule and a trembling but quietly confident faith we began with twelve priests. One of the twelve was Fr. George De Prizio who was visiting Ireland at the time and whom we had asked to lead us for the first week. Only the Lord knows how much help Fr. George gave us and what an inspiration his holiness and wit were to us all.

To be honest I was afraid that it would be too Charismatic to begin with and that priests who were not involved in the Renewal would be "put off" by it all. As it turned out those that the Lord sent were all men deep in his Holy Spirit; one with an extraordinary gift of prophesy through which the Lord spoke to us very powerfully during the two weeks that this priest remained with us. From the start it became clear that the Lord wanted to fill us with his Holy Spirit and with all the gifts and fruits of the Spirit. Priests who had not been in the Renewal would come up and say: "Father, if I had known beforehand that it was going to be Charismatic I would not have come but I am so glad I did." We could feel that Jesus was drawing us into His love and wanted us to accept and experience that love. Many words came to us in prophesy to this effect:

"Come to me and open your hearts to My Spirit. Listen to my voice and let my Spirit lead you today and I will fill you with My love. I have loved you with an everlasting love; why won't you come to My love."

At Mass He told us:

"My Children, My word will only grow where there is love. Open your hearts to Me. Do not hold back. Open your hearts to Me and I will fill them with my love in the Eucharist. You are My heart."

Every priest who came was amazed at the great spirit of peace and love which they felt. As one Dublin Diocesan Priest put it: "Many of us attending the Intercession had never met before, yet within hours of arriving you felt very much at one with your brothers in the priesthood." I remember one night we reflected on Jesus washing the Apostles feet. The exhortation of Jesus struck me as never before:

"If I then your Lord and Master have washed your feet, you should wash each others feet...Happiness will be yours if you behave accordingly" (John 13:17).

We experienced this happiness as we ministered to each other. Jesus guarantees this happiness to priests who minister to the needs of their brother priests. A beautiful thing happened to us on the second day of our Intercession when the Lord sent us a brother priest in a wheelchair who had for many years been suffering form multiple sclerosis. In his very presence he symbolized all that was paralysed and broken and helpless about so many of the priests whom we were praying for. He came to us on several occasions, during the month to be with us at prayer and at the Eucharist and every time he came all the priests present were deeply moved and some of us, feeling the weight of Christ's sorrow for His priests, were moved to tears. Later the Lord spoke to us in prophesy:

"Your tears are refreshment to My heart and I will refresh your brethren with My love."

Time and again our Lord drew our attention to the power we had received at ordination, His power, and told us not to be afraid to use it. He wanted us to be aware of our power to heal in His name. About this time He gave us a beautiful word::

"For lo My healing spirit shall overflow
like a river overflowing it's banks.
For lo my healing spirit shall come upon you
and you shall go to cleanse, to heal, to purify,
and My word upon your lips shall heal and cleanse,
and my word shall set My people free.
My word shall be your healing word
and your hands shall be My healing hands."

There were times especially during Mass and in the presence of the Blessed Sacrament exposed when we became so aware of our Lord's presence to us that many cast themselves to the ground overcome by the power of the living Lord. And always the inescapable conviction that the Lord wanted to prove His presence beyond all measure if only we would let Him be the Lord of our lives. In a word of gentle irony He said to us:

"Give me your glory and your power and I will give you My glory and My power."

Our daily schedule started out as a verbatim copy of the one in Frs. Judd and Kosicki's booklet, until we decided to modify it. We finished up with the following –

- 8 – 8.30am Morning Prayer from the Divine Office. We used to pause after each Psalm and share our thoughts and prayers. The same was done after Evening Prayer from 6pm to 6.30pm.

- 10 – 11.30am Was a period of common intercessory prayer for priests followed by a teaching. For the first week the teaching was given by Fr. George De Prizio and subsequently by one of ourselves or someone invited in especially for that purpose.

- 12 – 1.30pm Was set aside for Mass.
  For all of us each day the Mass was a glorious experience of being with Christ in Word and Sacrament. So much happened on so many occasions during Mass that to attempt to describe it would really be futile.

- 1.30 – 4.30pm Lunch at 1.30pm was followed by a period of solitude.

- 4.30 – 5.30pm We went off like the Disciples in twos for a period of one hour during which time we talked about what the priesthood meant to our lives, an experience which most of us found very helpful and enriching.

- 8.00pm We had another period of intercessory prayer. Most often this took the form of an ordinary prayer meeting. We would vary it by praying in the presence of the Blessed Sacrament exposed. On a few occasions we had the Stations of the Cross and Devotions centered on Our Lady and the Rosary. Once or twice, we broke into groups of four or five and prayed over each other in turn for whatever we wanted the Lord to give us anointing each other with Blessed oil. This type of experience of the priesthood and of ministering to each other, so new to most of us, touched us deeply by its simplicity, its tenderness and by the palpable love of Christ which flowed through it. It was as if Jesus was saying to us: "Let Me be the Centre of your lives and I will show you how easy it is for you to love one another."

- Officially everything ended at 9.30pm. At that time, we exposed the Blessed Sacrament in the Church so that anyone who wanted to could adore our Lord in prayer.

There were five Saturdays during the month and we had written to all the Prayer Groups in Ireland asking them to join in our Intercession and if possible to come to the College Chapel at All Hallows on Saturday evenings to take part in a public prayer meeting. Each week more people came so that on the final Saturday the Church was filled to overflowing. It showed us, if we ever needed it, just how much the people love the priesthood and care about their priests. Some of them actually thanked us for allowing them to come.

We had letters of encouragement and support from all kinds of places. The first and most deeply touching said: "You are in our Intercession here at Bethany as you begin your thirty days of Intercession." It was signed by George Kosicki and twenty-six of the priests at Bethany House of Intercession, Providence, Rhode Island. We were moved by their wonderful thoughtfulness. Fr. Michael Killeen who co-ordinated the Intercession held at Ros-on-Wey in England wrote to say that they had been praying for us. Mothers wrote to ask us to pray for their sons who were thinking of leaving the priesthood. A Columban Sister wrote from Jeju Island, Korea. She said: "You will not be able to see the fruit of your Intercession but many will benefit from it. During the month we will pray especially for all your intentions and with the heat here we will be able to do a little penance as well."

Priests who had spent some time with us wrote to tell us how it affected them. One described his eleven days as "the most wonderful days of communing with the Lord and being reassured by Him during the ministration of brother priests that I have ever experienced in all my life."

During the month the catering was done for us by half a dozen Daughters of Charity. One of them wrote about her reaction to the experience: "It was such a wonderful time for me that at times I thought that the Lord was getting confused and had come to the kitchens by mistake."

At the end we could hardly believe that the time had passed so quickly. We finished with Mass on August 15th, the Feast of Our Lady's Assumption into Heaven. It is difficult to write anything like an adequate account of such an experience as this. How can you describe the love of God. You can only experience it.

The Holy Spirit led us to pray for many priests all over the world often led by a brother-priest home on vacation from places as far away as the Philippines, Rhodesia, South Africa, and Australia. We prayed for our Bishops, for pastors, for missionaries, teachers, canon lawyers, seminary professors, for priests in prison, for priests at odds with the Church and for the very many brothers who had left the ministry altogether. And of course we did not forget to give praise and thanks to the Father for the great army of holy and zealous priests who preach the Good News of the Gospel to all nations.

One felt that the winter of our discontent was becoming, if not glorious summer, at least a kind of second spring. We were gathered together in one place and He had come to us in spite of the walls and the closed doors and had said:

"Peace be with you. Happy are those who have not seen and yet believe."

One thing is certain: what is true of two or three Christians gathered in the Lord's name is true beyond measure of priests. There were one hundred and twenty of us and our experience has left our hearts burning within us. Time and again He reminded us that we are His friends, that we have expected entirely too little from Him because we have relied too much on our own powers. We are living in a time of the special outpouring of the Holy Spirit on the Church.

During our month of prayer we received that Spirit:

".....not the spirit of slaves bringing fear into your lives again; it is the spirit of sons and it makes us cry out, 'Abba, Father!' The spirit himself and our spirit bear united witness that we are children of God. And if we are children we are heirs as well: heirs of God and coheirs with Christ, sharing his suffering so as to share his glory" (Romans 8:14-17).[1]

---

1. Fr. Kevin Scallon CM, *Report written of the first Intercession for Priests 16 July – 15 August 1976* (1976).

Chapter 3

Vessels of Clay

Some Thoughts On The Priesthood by Fr. Kevin Scallon CM

The priesthood as we know it in the Catholic Church was prefigured by the priesthood of the Old Testament and particularly the priesthood of Melkizidec, who came so suddenly into the life of the patriarch Abraham and on his behalf offered a sacrifice of bread and wine. So, when at the last supper Jesus took bread and wine he did something which had reference to all that had gone before in the Old Testament and all that was to come in this new convenant of his body and blood. As we know, Jesus took bread and wine, blessed it, and gave it to his disciples, saying to them, "This is my body...this is my blood...do this in memory of me". The words "in memory of me" refer most particularly to Jesus' passion, death, and resurrection, but they also refer to every moment in the life of Jesus. The Church's way of doing this in memory of Jesus is through the celebration of the Holy Eucharist. In the Eucharist, the Church remembers the totality of the life of Jesus, but in a most special way it makes present his passion, death, and glorious resurrection, in other words, the paschal mystery.

When Jesus at the last supper instituted the Holy Eucharist, he at the same time instituted the priestly ministry. We know that through baptism, everyone shares in the priesthood of Christ, but through the sacrament of the priesthood certain men are called by God and chosen by the Church to exercise the priesthood of Jesus on behalf of all of God's people. We understand from this that there is a significant difference between the universal priesthood of the baptized and the ministerial priesthood of those that receive the Sacrament of Holy Orders.

The supreme representative of Jesus Christ, the high priest in every diocese, is the bishop, who the successor of the apostles on whom Jesus conferred his own priesthood. The presbyters in the Church, the priests in your parish, share the priesthood of Christ on behalf of their bishop. As the Vatican Council states, "The function of the Bishop's ministry was handed over in a subordinate way to priests so that they might be appointed in the order of the priesthood and be co-workers of the Episcopal Order for the proper fulfillment of the apostolic mission that has been entrusted to it by Christ".

What we have to clearly understand in the Church is that even though there are many ordained to the priesthood, there is only one priesthood. The priesthood, as understood in the Catholic Church, is the priesthood of Jesus Christ. We see this very clearly illustrated for us during the celebration of Mass. During the Eucharistic prayer, the priest prays on behalf of the people, referring to God in the third person. But when it comes to the words of consecration, he uses the first person singular. He says "This is my body...this is my blood", using the very words of Jesus himself, because he is standing in the place of Jesus himself. The Vatican Counsel repeating the traditional teaching of the Church says that the priest acts *in persona Christi*, that is to say, in the person or in the place of Jesus himself. So that when we talk about priesthood in the Catholic Church, it must be clearly understood that we are referring to the one, the only, the unique, the eternal priesthood of our Lord Jesus Christ.

The priest acting in the person of Christ is ordained to proclaim the good news of the gospel, even as Jesus did who laid down his life for this very gospel. He is called upon to celebrate the sacred mysteries of the Eucharist and all of the sacraments on behalf of the whole Church.

As we know in the Church, this sacred ministry, this precious gift of Christ to the Church, is carried "in vessels of clay". The humanity and the sinfulness of the men who are called to this ministry is something that priests themselves must constantly be aware of. And yet, the priest, in virtue of his high calling, ought to be a man of God and ought to strive for outstanding holiness.

Today we are witnessing what amounts to a great apostasy in the Church, a rejection of the truth of Christ. This is seen very clearly in the reaction of many, even within the Church to the clear unambiguous teaching of the Supreme Pontiff. This onslaught on the Church by the forces of secularism and neo-paganism is particularly directed at those who are called to exercise the priestly ministry. That is why it is so important for people who love Jesus Christ, who love the Church, who reverence the priesthood, who revere the Blessed Eucharist and all of the other Sacraments, for them to pray earnestly for the protection and the sanctification of their own priests and of all who are called to this wonderful ministry of the Church.[1]

---

1. Fr. Kevin Scallon CM, *Article for Chicago Marian Center, March/April issue* (1995).

Chapter 4

Intercession for Priests: A Final Reflection

By Fr. Kevin Scallon CM

Why has it lasted so long? The Lord alone knows. I think it is because it has provided for many priests, a rock, a place of security where they can come and feel at home in their priesthood. It is a familiar place where psalms are sung and heard in a new way; where the divine therapist is encountered in the forgiveness of sin and the binding up of wounds; where there are no games and you don't have to be careful about what you say; where you can pray with and for each other. Perhaps it is all these things that draws so many us to come here year after year.

I thank the Father of all. I thank Jesus, our Eternal High Priest. I thank the Holy Spirit who never fails to teach us. I thank the Mother of God who is always present with us. I thank you for coming faithfully. I thank my Vincentian Superiors and confreres for their gentle approval and support. I especially thank the core group whose fidelity is beyond compare. I thank the countless brothers and sisters who have joined us each weekend and each year at Knock to pray for their priests. And, of course, I thank Sr. Briege McKenna OSC. Providentially, Sr. Briege came to see me for the first time on that fateful 16th of July. Her love for the Church and for the priesthood was then, as now, unconditional. Her gift of ministering to priests was even more striking, as so many of us have come to know.

I pray that the future of the *Intercession for Priests* will be as blessed as its past and that it will continue to be a source of strength and grace for many priests in the years to come. [1]

---

1. Fr. Kevin Scallon CM, *Reflection written for the 25th Jubilee of the Intercession for Priests* (2000).

Chapter 5
50 Years of Intercession for Priests
A Visual Celebration

The Intercession for Priests has been a long-standing annual program held in Ireland, England, Germany, and Poland. For over forty years, it has also served as the foundation for priests' retreats worldwide, inspiring spiritual renewal and support for clergy across the globe.

1970s - All Hallows, Dublin, Ireland

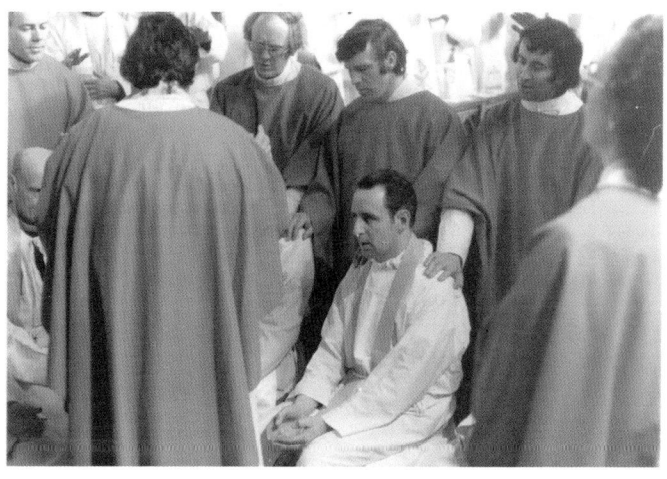

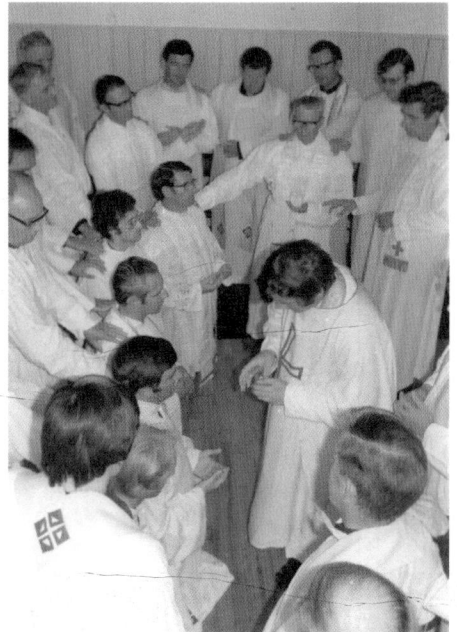

1970s - All Hallows, Dublin, Ireland

***

1985 - Taipei, Taiwan

1987 - All Hallows, Dublin, Ireland

1987 - All Hallows, Dublin, Ireland

1987 - Jos, Nigeria

1989 - Jos, Nigeria

1989 - Kumasi, Ghana

***

1990 - Mzuzu, Malawi

1991 - Perth, Australia

1991 - Armidale, Australia

RETREAT WITH FR. KEVIN SCALLON AND SR. BRIEGE McKENNA Apr. 5-10 1992

1992 - Ibaraki-Ken, Japan

1993 - Sao Paulo, Brazil

1993 - Cebu, Philippines

1993 - Having a bit of fun in Kiribati, Central Pacific Union

1993 - Kota Kinabalu, Malaysia

1994 - Tagaytay, Philippines

1995 - Baguio, Philippines

1995 - Magdalenka & Gostyn, Poland

1996 - Kundiawa, Papua New Guinea

1998 - Fukuoka City, Japan

1999 - Abu Dhabi, United Arab Emirates

1999 - Nairobi, Kenya

***

2000 - Kokstad, South Africa

2002 - Kuching, Sarawak, Malaysia

2005 - Rio de Janeiro, Brazil

2005 - Cikanyere, Indonesia

2005 - Bamenda, Cameroon

2005 - Having some more fun in Cameroon

2006 - Carabayllo, Peru

2006 - Vilnius, Lithuania

2007 - Wigratzbad, Germany

2007 - Lujan, Argentina

2008 - Florida

2008 - Pinkafeld, Austria

2008 - Malang, Java, Indonesia

2009 - Flores, Indonesia

2009 - Kosice, Slovakia

2009 - All Hallows, Dublin, Ireland

***

2010 - Enugu, Nigeria

2010 - Collevalenza, Italy

2010 - Loreto, Italy

2010 - Tierni, Italy

2010 - Flueli, Switzerland

2010 - Knock Shrine, Ireland

2010 - Brenna, Poland

2011 - Valle de Ángeles, Honduras

2011 - All Hallows, Dublin, Ireland

2011 - Buenos Aires, Argentina

2012 - Grodek n/Dunajcem, Poland

2013 - Lubuan Bajo, Flores, Indonesia

2013 - Brenna, Poland

2013 - Loyola, Spain

2014 - Lima, Peru

2014 - Leeds, England

2015 - All Hallows, Dublin, Ireland

2015 - Kalwaria Zebrzydowska, Poland

2016 - Marienfried, Bavaria, Germany

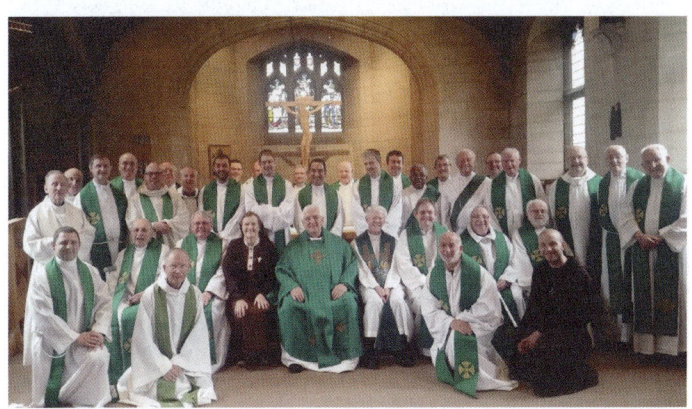

2016 - Leeds, England

2016 - Intercession's 41st and last year at All Hallows, Dublin, Ireland

2016 - Kalwaria Zebrzydowska, Poland

2017 - Máriabesnyo, Gödöllo, Hungary

2017 - Kalwaria Zebrzydowska, Poland

2017 - Zeliv, Czech

2017 - Marienfried, Bavaria, Germany

2017 - Intercession's first year at St. Patrick's College, Maynooth, Ireland

2018 - Leeds, England

2019 - Marienfried, Bavaria, Germany

***

2022 - Buenos Aires, Argentina

2022 - Belo Horizonte, Brazil

2022 - Leeds, England

2022 - Marienfried, Bavaria, Germany

2022 - Brenna, Poland

2023 - Toronto, Canada

2023 - Marienfried, Bavaria, Germany

2023 - Maynooth, Ireland

2023 - Brenna, Poland

2023 - Jakarta, Indonesia

2023 - Singapore

2023 - Taipei, Taiwan

2024 - Lima, Peru

2024 - Fatima, Portugal

2024 - Leeds, England

2024 - Marienfried, Bavaria, Germany

2024 - Rigas, Latvia

2024 - Maynooth, Ireland

2024 - Brenna, Poland

2024 - Krosno, Poland

2024 - East Flores, Indonesia

2024 - Cordoba, Argentina

Printed in Dunstable, United Kingdom